I0795106

© Hasan Can Balcioglu | Dreamstime.com

The Garden Island

Known as the Garden Island for its lush rainforests teeming with bold flowers and verdant plants, its emerald valleys and jagged cliffs, its winding rivers and cascading waterfalls, Kaua'i is the oldest island and fourth largest in the Hawaiian Island chain.

The island's color is a regal purple and its flowers come from the endemic mokihana tree.

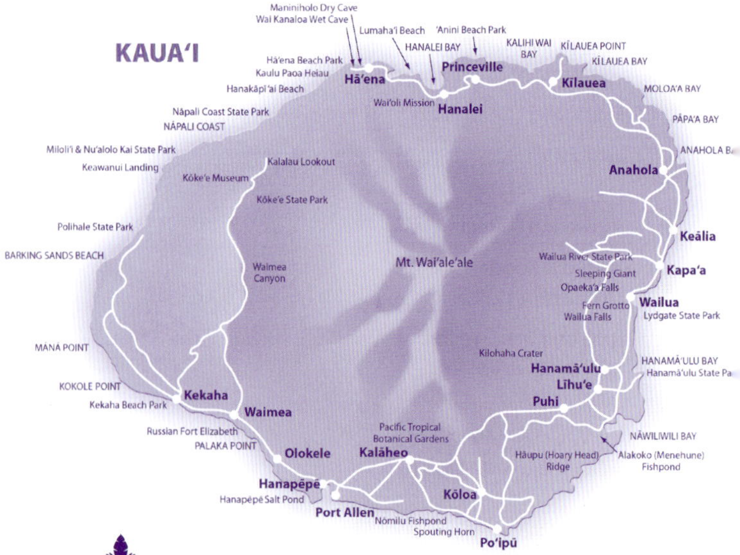

Aloha!

ALOHA
is the spiritual key.

ALOHA is the familiar
Hawaiian greeting and farewell.

ALOHA signifies the sentiments of
affection, sympathy, kindness, and love.

ALOHA is the spirit of friendliness and
hospitality–the essence of the Hawaiian culture.

ALOHA represents the Hawaiians' love of life–
their art of living. For their wealth was not in
aggressive accumulation of things, but in their
joy in sharing and giving.

ALOHA to all of you who enjoy and appreciate
Hawai'i–its beauty, its people, and its spirit.

LaRue W. Piercy
Kailua-Kona, Hawai'i

Contents

UNIQUE KAUA'I

Only State With...

- Nā Pali Coastline.
- Waimea Canyon, the Grand Canyon of the Pacific.
- Hawai'i's biggest rivers; Hanalei, Wailua, Waimea, Kalihiwai.
- Limahuli Gardens.
- Barking Sands, the longest beach in Hawai'i.
- Bird species only ever found on Kaua'i; Kaua'i 'akialoa *(Akialoa stejnegeri)*, Kaua'i 'ākepa *(Loxops caeruleirostris)*, Kaua'i 'amakihi *(Chlorodrepanis stejnegeri)*, Kaua'i 'elepaio *(Chasiempis sclateri)*, Kaua'i 'ō'ō *(Moho braccatus)*. Besides the 'elepaio, 'amakihi, and 'ākepa these birds are now extinct.

KAUA'I STATISTICS

Population

- Estimated County population (including Ni'ihau) in 2021 was 73,454.
- The population of Ni'ihau in 2020 was 84.

Land

- Kaua'i County—629.8 sq. miles (1637.5 sq. km.) of land and inland water areas.
- Kaua'i Island—555 sq. miles (1443 sq. km.) of land and inland water areas. Kaua'i is 33 miles (53 km.) in length and 25 miles (40 km.) in width.
- Kaua'i has 90 miles (144 km.) of general coastline.
- Ni'ihau Island—71 sq. miles (184.6 sq. km.) of land and inland water areas. Ni'ihau is 18 miles (29 km.) in length and 6 miles (10 km.) in width.

Population Centers

- The county seat and main town is at Līhu'e. The main town of Ni'ihau is Pu'uwai. Other main population centers on Kaua'i are located at Kapa'a, Wailua Homesteads, Hanamā'ulu, Kalaheo, Waimea, and Hanalei.

- Highway Distances Līhu'e to Ha'ena is 38 miles (61 km.)
- Līhu'e to Po'ipū is 12 miles (19 km.).
- Līhu'e to Mānā is 33 miles (53 km.).
- Līhu'e to Kalalau Lookout at Kōke'e is 42 miles (66 km.).

KAUA'I'S PEOPLE

ETHNIC POPULATION, 2010

Caucasian	26.6%	17,875
Filipino	14.8%	9,934
Japanese	9.2%	6,167
Native Hawaiian	9.4%	6,290
Chinese	3.3%	2,215
Korean	0.5%	335
Black or African American	0.6%	400
Samoan	0.5%	335
Vietnamese	0.5%	335
Marshallese	0.1%	54
Other Races	4.3%	2790
Mixed (Two or more races)	6.8%	4,408

RELIGIONS

DENOMINATIONS, 2010	
Protestant	28.8%
Roman Catholic	21%
Unaffiliated	22.4%
Buddhist	4.5%
Mormon	3.6%
Jehovah's Witness	> 1%
Other faiths	3.19%

PRECIOUS LAND

Kaua'i is an attractive investment opportunity and firms and individuals continue to buy large swaths of land. Although these statistics reflect 2013 land ownership, figures are constantly shifting. In 2022 Brue Baukol Capital Partners purchased over 18,000 acres of land, surpassing Alexander & Baldwin in terms of pure land ownership.

359,872 ACRES	
cropland	5,467 acres
grazing land	36,500 acres
forests	155,000 acres
urban and built-up	12,100 acres
misc./non-farmland	57,621 acres

WHO OWNS THE LAND? (2017)	
State government	136,025 acres
Robinson Family	50,614 acres
Grove Farm	33,294 acres
Alexander & Baldwin	2,1016 acres

Govt. State DHHL (Depart. of Hawaiian Homelands)	19,515 acres
Kamehameha Schools	10,872 acres
Princeville Dev. LLC	6,506 acres
Robinson B.B.	4,272 acres
Cornerstone Hawaii	4,265 acres
Mahaulepu Farm LLC	3,835 acres
E.A. Knudsen Trust	3,561 acres
Govt. Federal	3,437 acres
W.H. Rice	1,917 acres
Canpartner Realty	1,490 acres
D.R. Campion	1,398 acres
Bette Midler	1,393 acres
Halaulani Condominium	1,387 acres
Haupu Land Co.	1,386 acres
National Tropical Botanical Gardens	1,236 acres
Jurassic Kahili Ranch	1,182 acres
Share No. 1	1,120 acres
Visionary LLC	1,018 acres
Govt. County of Kauai	873 acres

AGRICULTURE

Seed production–14,255 acres on Kaua'i (2020).

- Seed production increasingly has become Kaua'i's number one agricultural business after the 2010 closure of the Gay & Robinson Sugar Plantation in Kaumakani. This plantation was the last working sugar mill in Hawai'i.
- Crops grown for seed production in Kaua'i include corn, sunflowers, soybeans, and various vegetable seeds.

Production–29.6 million pounds of corn a year, 2.7 million pounds of soy a year, and 3.3 million pounds of sunflower seeds.

Controversy–Seed production on Kaua'i employs biotech research in growing genetically modified seeds; some local residents have health concerns.

Players–Monsanto, Syngenta, DuPont-Pioneer, Dow Chemical and BASF (2016).

Taro–Hawai'i's original root vegetable staple is still

grown extensively on Kaua'i. In 2020, Kaua'i planted 546 acres of taro, by far the most planted in the state.

Coffee–Kaua'i's rich soil makes for delicious coffee and dates back to the nineteenth century. In 2019, 2.7 million pounds were produced which amounted to $7.8 million in sales. Kauai Coffee is the largest coffee grower in the United States.

Diversified crops–Emerging as a farming community, Kaua'i continues to produce diversified crops, farmer-run "food forests," and permaculture farms, especially on the lush North Shore.

Livestock–Over $12.6 million worth produced in 2020. Notable ranches include Makaweli Meat Co., Princeville Ranch, Kauai Ranch, and Rancher's Daughter's Reserve. While not every ranch on Kaua'i practices grass-fed livestock raising, the economy is shifting towards a Kaua'i market for grass-fed beef which can be found more readily on the island.

COST OF LIVING

One of the most remote places on planet Earth, the cost of living on Kaua'i remains high due to factors such as shipping costs, a small percentage of habitable land, and complicated building permit procedures which make it expensive to live on Kaua'i.

Kaua'i's overall cost of living (housing, food, transportation, utilities, health care, misc. expenses such as clothing, services, entertainment), not including state and local taxes, is 54.6% higher than the U.S. average.

Groceries cost 67.6% higher than on the U.S. mainland.

Housing costs 134.7% higher than on the U.S. mainland with a median home cost of $858,900. The average rent per month for a:

- studio apartment: $1,440
- one bedroom: $1,630
- two bedroom: $2,150
- three bedroom: $2,880
- four bedroom: $3,510

Utilities cost 99.4% higher than on the U.S. mainland.

Transportation costs 11.5% less than on the U.S. mainland.

Kaua'i's unemployment rate (2022): 4.1%

KAUA'I COUNTY TAX RATES:

Sales Tax Rate:	4%	U.S. average is 7.3%
Income tax rate:	8.3%	U.S. average is 4.6%

The average income of a Kaua'i County resident is $27,079 a year. The U.S. average is $28,555 a year.

The median household income of a Kaua'i County resident is $62,946 a year. The U.S. average is $53,482 a year.

© Sarah Fields | Dreamstime.com

❀ Visiting Kaua'i ❀

WHAT TO EXPECT

- Daily passing showers—Expect warm, tropical temperatures, but always prepare for rain! Kaua'i is one of the wettest places on earth, and rain is a daily experience on the island.
- Azure oceans capped with shell-covered white sand beaches expanding into verdant wetland farms crowned with lush mysterious mountains.
- Unique features—Waimea Canyon, navigable natural waterways, Polihale—a 17 mile long white sand beach, the epic Nā Pali Coastline, Hanalei taro fields.
- Incredible beachfront properties with stereoscopic views of waterfall covered mountains.
- A slow and rural lifestyle; a great place to relax.
- Exciting outdoor activities—sailing, surfing, water skiing, kite boarding, cliff diving, fishing, hiking, hunting, horseback riding, diving.
- International cast of transient characters.
- The Garden Island—Kaua'i is GREEN—be sure to visit Allerton & McBryde Gardens on the South

Shore and Limahuli Garden and Preserve on the gorgeous North Shore. They are part of the National Tropical Botanical Gardens system and a must visit on Kaua'i.

VISITOR ARRIVALS TO KAUA'I COUNTY (2021)

Total	Domestic	International
813,647	80,658	5,990

AVERAGE DAILY VISITORS (2021)

Total	Domestic	International
19,194	19,026	168

Number of hotels:	341
Number of hotel units:	7,612
Number of condominiums:	16
Number of condominium units:	1,548

Hotel room occupancy (2021):	58.5%
Average daily room rate (2021):	$324.19

NUMBER OF NATIONAL AND STATE HISTORIC SITES (2022)

Listed Hawai'i Register:	81
Listed National Register:	40

HOW FAR FROM HOME (OR SOMEPLACE ELSE)

LĪHU'E TO:	MILES	FLIGHT TIME
San Francisco	2,450.41	4h, 47m
Los Angeles	2,628.58	5h, 1m
Portland	2,627.26	5h, 45 m
Seattle	2,706.29	5h, 18m
Las Vegas	2,821.93	6h, 9m
Vancouver, B.C.	2,729.54	5h, 58m
Guam	3,692.15	7h, 54m
Tokyo	3,738.41	7h, 59m
Chicago	4,304.14	9h, 7m
Auckland, N.Z.	4,402.23	9h, 16m
Washington, D.C.	4,885.41	10h, 17m
Miami	4,936.72	10h, 23m
New York	4,899.80	10h, 32m
Sydney	5,041.82	10h, 34m
Manila	5,185.73	10h, 53m
Hong Kong	5,431.79	11h, 23m

❀ WEATHER? ❀

Almost Perfect, but Anticipate Rain!

- How's the weather here?–Expect sunny skies, warm breezes, a cool sea, and typically passing rain showers in the afternoon–but sometimes it rains a lot–in 2018 a storm on the North Shore of Kaua'i dumped fifty inches of rainfall in twenty-four hours–a world record.
- More rain!–Kaua'i's Mount Wai'ale'ale (rippling water in Hawaiian) holds a record of being one of the wettest places on earth–it averages around 450 inches of rain a year!
- Seasons–Kaua'i has two seasons: dry and wet. Although always warm, Kaua'i almost always has heavy rain through late fall/winter months and dries out late spring and into fall.
- Hurricanes generally pass by–Dot hit Kaua'i, August 1959–Iwa hit Kaua'i and O'ahu November 23, 1982, $234 million damage–'Iniki hit Kaua'i and O'ahu September 1992, almost $2 billion in damages.

- Rainfall records—Wai'ale'ale, Kaua'i, one of the "Wettest Spots on Earth," has recorded over 600 inches/year. Today a computerized rain gauge keeps track of rainfall.

❀ FAVORITE ATTRACTIONS ❀

ATTENDANCE IN 2019	
Waimea Canyon	1,120,000
Nā Pali Coast State Wilderness Park	1,000,000
Wailua Falls	600,000
Kīlauea Point National Wildlife Refuge	400,000
Hanalei Bay	300,000

OTHER SPECIAL ATTRACTIONS	
Po'ipū Beach Park	300,000
Limahuli Garden and Preserve	150,000
Kauai Coffee Company	150,000
Kōke'e State Park	100,000
Kaua'i Museum	75,000

Some Beauty Spots

ʻŌpaekaʻa Falls Lookout–convenient stop to view the 151-foot tall, 40-foot wide waterfall.

Polihale State Park–secluded beach requiring four-wheel drive access; large sand dunes as high as 100 feet. Good for camping; not for inexperienced swimmers.

Kīlauea Lighthouse–spectacular view from a 180-foot ocean bluff; best place to view seabirds.

Hanalei Valley Lookout–view of beautiful, verdant mountains with waterfalls overlooking Hanalei Valley's patchwork of taro fields.

Kilohana Vista–breathtaking views of the beautiful Wainiha Valley and Kauaʻi's North Shore at the end of Alakaʻi Swamp Trail.

Māhāʻulepū Heritage Trail–a 2-mile coastal trail that runs along some of the most dramatic cliffs on south Kauaʻi.

The Russian Fort–the last remaining Russian fort on the islands, built in 1817; National Historic Landmark.

Kēʻē Beach–crescent-shaped beach on the Nā Pali Coast.

HAWAIIAN HOLIDAYS AND CELEBRATIONS

Prince Kūhiō Day–March 26, honoring birthday of Prince Jonah Kūhiō Kalniana'ole, nephew of Queen Li-li'uokalani and Republican delegate to Congress in 1902-22. Special celebration held at Prince Kūhiō Beach Park, Po'ipū, Kaua'i.

Lei Day–May 1, Hawai'i's pageantry version of May Day. A special celebration is held at Hanalei School on Kaua'i's North Shore.

Kamehameha Day–June 11, honoring founder of Kingdom of Hawai'i.

Admission Day–Third Friday in August, commemorating Hawai'i's admission to the Union, August 21, 1959.

Merrie Monarch Festival–Hilo in April. Week-long festivities and popular hula contests attract dancers and spectators from all islands.

Koloa Plantation Days–A ten-day festival held in July celebrating Kaua'i's plantation heritage.

Waimea Town Celebration—A festival lasting a week in February honoring the history of Waimea Town.

© Kilmermedia | Dreamstime.com

Hawai'i Food and Wine Festival—Held on multiple islands, this food and wine tasting event is not to be missed on Kaua'i. Sample the best local fare the island has to offer.

Queen Emalani Festival on Kaua'i—Held in Kōke'e, this festival pays homage to Queen Emma, King Kamehameha IV's wife. Expect hula, horseback pageantry, and a taste of real Hawai'i.

❀ NONE HERE! ❀

Happy Omissions

- Snakes
- Rabies—strict quarantine on incoming animals
- Cholera, malaria, small pox, yellow fever
- Billboards to spoil your view
- Hurricanes (seldom)
- Daylight Savings Time—no changing of the clocks in Hawai‘i
- Car horns—most people drive with aloha and rarely use their car horn
- Private beaches—all beaches in the islands are public

Also to be missed

- Grass skirts—hula skirts have ti leaves. Hawaiian women wore tapa skirts (pā‘ū)
- Hummingbirds—cross-pollination of pineapple blossoms would develop unwanted seeds in fruit
- Squirrels, racoons, chipmunks
- Many mainland chain retail stores and restaurants

FREE KAUA‘I ENTERTAINMENT

© Abigail Warick | Dreamstime.com

- Old Kapa‘a Town First Saturday Art Walk. Kapa‘a town's Art Walk features live music, artisans, street food.
- Hanapēpē Art Night–Every Friday night, wander Hanapēpē town, bustling galleries, shops, restaurants.
- Eo e Emalani i Alaka‘i–The Queen Emalani festival in Kōke‘e features live music, traditional hula, and a reenactment of a historical moment on Kaua‘i– Queen Emma's 1871 visit to Koke‘e & Alaka‘i Swamp.

COME SWIM KAUA'I
...BUT WHEN IN DOUBT DON'T GO OUT!

Kaua'i's pristine shorelines present warm and inviting waters, but sometimes hidden under a smooth ocean surface are strong rip tides—currents of water flowing swiftly out to sea. Always seek local advice; Kaua'i is an island of water people, and most locals are happy to help out or point you in a safer direction. Dangerous shore break, hidden currents, and deceptively calm water that can become instantly dangerous and lead to many spinal injuries, drownings, and deaths in the waters here.

When in doubt, don't go out. Know where you are, always keep your eyes toward the ocean when you're in the surf, and know your limits—don't become another victim of a broken neck, drowning, or permanent injury.

❀ MUSIC OF THE HEART ❀

Larry Rivera—Born in 1931, Larry Rivera was a true Kaua'i icon. In 1951, he began working at the historic Coco Palms Resort in Wailua as a bartender, dishwasher, and server before eventually landing a residency as a performing musician. In 1961, a scene in Elvis Presley's film *Blue Hawai'i* was shot at Coco Palms and Larry and Elvis became friends. Elvis even performed backup vocals on stage for Larry's show. Larry lived for performing. He continued his act until he recently passed away in 2023. His aloha spirit-fueled personality and *joie de vivre* will always be remembered on Kaua'i.

Israel Kamakawiwo'ole—Perhaps Hawai'i's most beloved musical artist of all time, Israel Kamakawiwo'ole, also know as IZ or Bruddah Iz, was born in Honolulu, on May 20, 1959. Bruddah Iz traces his ancestry back to Ni'ihau, "the Forbidden Island," visible from Kaua'i's West Coast. His mother, Evangeline Keale Kamakawiwo'ole, was pure Hawaiian and born there. Kamakawiwo'ole's pure voice and authentic music stands the test of time as some of the best Hawaiian music worldwide, especially with his timeless covers of "Somewhere Over the Rainbow," and "What A Wonderful World," and his dreamy original composition "White Sandy Beach of Hawai'i."

Carlos Andrade–Native to Kaua'i, Carlos exemplified the Hawaiian spirit through musical creativity, cultural awareness, and a warm and kind attitude full of welcome and aloha. Andrade's life reads like a novel; born Carlos Lawrence Andrade on May 29, 1944 in Kīlauea, Kaua'i, Andrade went on to sail on the famous *Hōkūle'a,* surfed, composed songs and released albums, had his music covered by the likes of Hawaiian music legend Gabby Pahanui (check out "Moonlight Lady"), lived off-grid, and eventually went back to school in his forties and became the head of the Hawaiian studies department at UH Mānoa on O'ahu. Carlos passed away in 2022 in his hometown of Kīlauea, leaving behind a truly remarkable legacy of music, cultural heritage, and timeless songs about Kaua'i and Hawai'i.

SUGGESTED GIFTS FROM KAUA'I

Clothing–Aloha shirts, bikinis, locally-made fashion, hats, T-shirts.

Jewelry–Ni'ihau shell lei (a unique craft to Kaua'i and Ni'ihau), sunrise shells, puka shell necklaces, black kukui nut necklaces.

Crafts–Lauhala (a traditional Hawaiian method of interweaving hala leaves) bags, mats, and other handcrafted items; photographic prints, paintings, and sculptures.

Memories–Photo albums, journals, coffee table books.

Produce–Taro, coconuts, 'ulu (breadfruit), Kaua'i coffee, mangoes.

Flowers–Orchids and anthuriums–only buy plants specially prepped for travel intra/outer state.

LEI OF KAUA'I

Lei Mokihana and lei maile are commonly associated with Kaua'i in chants and legends. Mokihana is officially named as Kaua'i's lei and is endemic to Kaua'i. Mokihana *(Pelea anisata)* is found in Kaua'i's highland forests at 1,200 to 4,200 feet above sea level.

Lei Mokihana–Anise-scented, round fruits of the mokihana tree, strung through center of the berry, prized for fragrant, forest scent. Mokihana berries can burn the skin of wearers.

Maile *(Alyxia olivaeformis)*–Possibly the first forest plant used for lei making. Kaua'i maile is round and with small leaves. Maile and mokihana are often interlaced with laua'e *(Microsorium scolopendria)* leaves.

Limu pahapaha *(Ulva fascitata)*–A seaweed lei, a floral sign that one had visited Polihale, made from seaweed gathered at Polihale at low tide.

TAKING AWAY PLANTS, FRUITS, AND FLOWERS

© Phyllis D. Peterson | Dreamstime.com

- **No restrictions**–ripe coconut, pineapple, macadamia nuts, flowers–except for gardenias, jade, mauna loa, any pea family
- **Must be fumigated**–avocado, banana, lychee, papaya; fumigated fruit available at airport and some dealers
- **Mango**–must be pitted, frozen, or cooked
- **No plants in soil**
- **Orchids**–shops carry pre-inspected plants
- **No citrus**–all items checked at Airport Agricultural Inspection

LANGUAGE

Standardized by missionaries in 1820s, only twelve-letter alphabet; five vowels, seven consonants: h, k, l, m, n, p, w.

Pronunciation—Vowels

a–ah–as in hale (house)–hah-lay
e–ay–as in kāne (man)–kah-nay
i–ee–as in ipo (sweetheart)-eepoh
o–oh–as in ʻono (good)–oh-noh
u–ue–as in pūpū (snack)–pooh-pooh

Common Words

Activities

hana–work
hui-club, organization
hukilau–group net fishing
kōkua–help
lomilomi–massage

Clothing

haori–Japanese coat
holokū-gown
lavalava-Samoan skirt
malo-loincloth
muʻumuʻu–long, loose dress
pāpale-hat
pāʻū–sarong-type skirt

Conditions

hoʻomalimali–flattery, sweet talk

huhū–anger
pilikia-trouble
wikiwiki–fast, hurry

Descriptions

akamai–clever, smart
auwe–alas
nani–beautiful
nui–big
ʻono–delicious
pau–done, finished
pupule–crazy

Directions

kona–leeward, south, south wind
makai–toward sea
mauka–toward mountain

People

aliʻi–chief, royalty
haole–white person; foreigner
kahuna–priest in old Hawaiʻi, expert practitioner
kamaʻāina–native-born or long-time resident
kāne-man
keiki–child, little one
kupuna-grandparent, ancestor
malihini–stranger, foreigner
paniolo–cowboy
tūtū–grandmother
wahine-woman

Religion

akua-god
amakua–family god
Kanaloa–god of deep sea
Kāne–giver of life
Kū–main god
lani-heaven
Lono–god of agriculture
mana–spirit, power
Pele–goddess of volcano

Things

'a'ā–rough, stony lava
hale–house
hīmeni–missionary hymns
hula–a dance
imu–underground oven
kāhili–feather-decorated royal standard
kai-sea
lānai–porch
lau–leaf
lua–hole, depression, toilet
mele–song, anthem, or chant
pāhoehoe–smooth or ropey lava
pua–flower
puka–hole, opening
pūne'e–couch
wai–water

Expressions

da kine (pidgin)–whachamacallit
Hau'oli lā hānau–Happy Birthday
Hauoli Makahiki Hou–Happy New Year
Mele Kalikimaka–Merry Christmas
mahalo nui–many thanks
Pehea 'oe?–How are you?

Natural History

KAUA'I'S WATERFALLS, MOUNTAINS, AND RIDGES

SIGNIFICANT WATERFALLS	
Waipo'o (Waimea Canyon)	800 feet/243 meters
'Awini (Waimea Canyon)	480 feet/146 meters
Hinalele (Wainiha Valley)	280 feet/85 meters
Kapaka Nui (Makaleha Mountains)	280 feet/85 meters
Manawaiopuna (Kāhili Mountain)	280 feet/85 meters
Wailua (Wailua Valley)	80 feet/24 meters
'Ōpaeka'a (Nounou Mountain)	40 feet (sheer drop)/12 meters

SIGNIFICANT MOUNTAINS AND RIDGES

Kawaikini Peak (the multitudinous water) at 5,243 feet/1,590 meters: Kaua'i's highest peak, located about

three-quarters-of-a-mile south of Wai'ale'ale.

Wai'ale'ale Peak (rippling water) 5,148 feet/1,561 meters: Kaua'i's landmark peak stands at the center of the island.

Nāmolokama (the interweaving bound fast) 4,421 feet/1,340 meters: Tallest peak in Hanalei Valley. Rare native plants are found at its plateau.

Kilohana Lookout (lookout point) 4,030 feet/1,222 meters: Offers spectacular view of Nā Pali, Wainiha Valley, and the north shore from the northwest tip of the Alaka'i Swamp at the end of the Alaka'i Swamp Trail.

Kalalau Lookout (the straying) 4,000 feet/1,219 meters: Spectacular lookout above Nā Pali's Kalalau Valley near end of Kōke'e Road.

Puu-ka-Pele (Hill of Pele) 3,662 feet/1,110 meters: Peak above Waimea Canyon where Pele departed Kaua'i.

Makaleha Mountains (eyes looking about as in wonder or admiration) 3,225 feet/ 978 meters: A mountain range behind Kapa'a and Anahola. Peak at Wēkiu • Kahili Peak (feather standard) 3,089 feet/936 meters: Mountainous backdrop to Kalāheo and Kīpū.

Namahana 2,814 feet/853 meters: Landmark mountain mauka of Kīlauea and Kalihiwai.

Hā'upu Range (probably named after a kahu ali'i from Kaua'i who threw a stone across Ka'ie'iewaho Channel toward O'ahu mistaking a gathering for a fishing tournament for invaders) 2,297 feet/696 meters: Also known as Hoary Head Range.

Kalalea Ridge (prominent) 1,946 feet/ 590 meters: It rises mauka of 'Aliomanu and is famous for its Hole in the Mountain, which collapsed in early 1980s. Also known as the Anahola Mountains. Peak at Pu'u Ehu.

Kamali'i Ridge (children) 1,736 feet/527 meters: Towering vertical peak directly mauka of Kapa'a and Kapahi.

Makana (gift) 1,280 feet/388 meters: Distinctive peak towering above Kē'ē Beach. It is a landmark when viewed from Hanalei and Princeville, dubbed Bali Hai in the film South Pacific.

Nounou Ridge (throwing) 1,247 feet/378 meters: Also known as Sleeping Giant. It is located above 'Ōpaeka'a Falls and Wailua Homesteads.

Kilohana Crater (lookout point) 1,133 feet/343 meters: Volcanic crater mauka of Līhu'e.

Kālepa Ridge Trail 709 feet/215 meters: Eroded mauka ridge runs from Hanamā'ulu to Fern Grotto and Wailua River.

KAUA'I'S BIRDS

More birds have become extinct in Hawai'i than in any other area of the world–twenty-six species lost, twenty-seven more are threatened by changes in natural habitats, forest destruction, cats, and humans.

The largest population of nesting birds in the state–Kīlauea Point National Wildlife Refuge, on the North Shore of Kaua'i, serves as a pristine cliffside nesting area for a diverse array of seasonal and year-round birds such as albatross, golden plover, tropicbirds, shearwater, red-footed and brown booby, and the nēnē goose.

Introduced Species

Brazilian cardinal–introduced in the 1930s; red head, bluish-gray back, white below.

California quail–brought to Hawai'i as a gift to Kamehameha in 1818; a small gray and brown game bird.

Cardinal–from about 1929.

Chukar–brought to Hawai'i as a game bird in 1923.

Dove–small barred from Malaysia, 1922; large spotted, before 1900.

English sparrow–in coastal areas before 1970.

House finch–from before 1970.

Mynah bird–from India, 1865.

Pheasant–from China, about 1865.

Java sparrow–from about 1865.

Skylark–1870.

Mejiro, warbling white-eye–from Japan, 1929.

Native Birds

Nēnē goose–Hawai'i's state bird, the nēnē nearly went extinct; flocks of up to 25,000 or more geese roamed the Hawaiian islands. This rarest goose in the world's population eventually dwindled to less than thirty in 1967 due to hunting and introduced predators: mongoose (they never made it to Kaua'i, thankfully), rats, feral cats, and dogs. The population now holds steady over 3,000 statewide due to the Endangered Species Act.

Hawaiian hawk ('Io)–Only on Hawai'i, the Big Island.

Short-eared owl (Pueo)–All main islands.

Tropicbirds–Catch them on Kaua'i beaches and valleys, especially between March-October.

Migratory Visitors

Gull, Plover, Sandpiper, Shearwater, Blue-winged teal

Bird Species Unique to Kauaʻi

While many of the bird species unique to Kauaʻi have become extinct, the following species still remain in the wild on Kauaʻi. These species once lived island-wide, but today they remain confined to a limited area of Kōkeʻe; the mountainous high-elevation area of Kauaʻi. While they sometimes wander, most of these ultra-rare birds can be typically found in the confines of the Alakaʻi Plateau. These species developed in isolation on Kauaʻi much like the diverse species of the Galapagos islands and are unique natural gems that conservationists fight to preserve on Kauaʻi.

ʻAkekeʻe ***(Loxops Caeruleirostris)***–a small green-yellow honeycreeper with a black face.

ʻAkikiki ***(Oreomystis Bairdi)***–a gray and white honeycreeper, the ʻAkikiki's population is in decline as its habitat decreases; 454 individuals reported remaining in the wild in 2018.

ʻAnianiau ***(Hemignathus Parvus)***–the smallest of the honeycreepers in Hawaiʻi, the ʻAnianiau is only found on

Kaua'i and is recognizable from it's bright green or yellow color and small size.

'I'iwi ***(Drepanis Coccinea*****)**–this unique red and black bird with a long curved beak can be found throughout the Hawaiian islands but is most common on Kaua'i; its red feathers were used traditionally for feathered helmets and capes. Their population on Kaua'i as of 2018 was 1855, which is in decline.

Kaua'i 'Amakihi ***(Chlorodrepanis Stejnegeri)***–an olive colored honeycreeper with a black line between its eyes and distinctly downward curving beak. The Kaua'i 'Amakihi is unique to Kaua'i and was reported to have a population of 51,817 in 2000; recent surveys show a dramatic decline to less then 7,000 birds in 2018.

Kaua'i 'Elepaio ***(Chasiempis Sandwichensis Sclateri)***–this diminutive brown and gray flycatcher can be found in high elevation and was once considered an 'aumakua, or ancestral guiding spirit, to Hawaiian wa'a (canoe) builders.

Puaihoi ***(Myadestes Palmeri)***–also known as the Small Kaua'i Thrush, this gray bird is a forager that eats native fruits and insects; population is unknown and being actively studied; scientists fear for its continued existence due to predatory rats.

ANIMALS

Feral domestic animals–introduced in the nineteenth century–cows, pigs, goats, sheep, and black tail deer–lots of game for hunters on Kaua'i.

Dogs–brought to Kaua'i by the original Polynesian settlers.

Rats–highly invasive and detrimental to the native bird population.

Bats–a native bat species, the Hawaiian hoary bat (*lasiurus semotus,* or 'ōpe'ape'a in Hawaiian). This diminutive fruit eating bat is extremely rare, only comes out at dusk, and is on the endangered species list.

NATIVE PLANTS

Hawai'i has the highest percentage of endemic (found no where else) plants in the world: 96% here before the Polynesians came, 4% indigenous to other Pacific islands. Scientists have identified more than 1,360 native plant species. At least half of the U.S.'s threatened and endangered plants grow in the Hawaiian Islands, which compromises only about 2% of the whole country's land surface area. This decline in the native plant population is due to feral animals–wild pigs, goats, sheep, cats, dogs, cattle–and invasive plant species such as liliko'i (passionfruit), ginger, bamboo, guava, albizia, lantana, guinea grass, and increasingly more species.

On Kaua'i alone, scientists from the National Tropical Botanical Garden have identified 255 unique endemic plants. In the state of Hawai'i, Kaua'i ranks number one in terms of endemic species and species diversity, most likely due to the isolated nature of the island and its age (Kaua'i is the oldest island in the state, almost 4.4 million years older than the newest island in the state: Hawai'i, also known as the Big Island).

As Kaua'i's pristine forests continue to be decimated by invasive species, it is important for visitors and locals alike to be aware of what plants they may be carrying on their pants or shoes, to responsibly spay and neuter their pets to keep feral cat/dog populations down, and to be aware of the ecological footprint everyone leaves when stepping on the island of Kaua'i.

A Few Ultra-Rare Endangered Plants from Kaua'i

Nani wai'ale'ale ***(Viola kauaiensis var. wahiawaensis)***–This small bog violet is a perennial herb with white to purple flowers and heart-shaped leaves and can only be found in one place in the world–Kanaele Bog, in the uplands of Kaua'i's south side.

Koki'o ke'oke'o ***(Hibiscus waimeae)***–A hibiscus with a white flower, only found in the Waimea Canyon.

Pa'iniu ***(Astelia waialealae)***–This small herb has silvery sword-shaped leaves and can be found only in the Alaka'i Swamp, a bog high a top Kaua'i. There are only twenty-six plants left in the world.

'Āwikiwiki ***(Canavalia napaliensis)***–Located only on Kaua'i's northwestern Nā Pali coastline, this small flowering pea plant is limited to a population of around 200 plants today.

Hau kuahiwi ***(Hibiscadelphus distans)***–This small tree with round, heart-shaped leaves can only be found in the Koai'e Canyon, a tributary deep within Waimea Canyon. There are only twenty wild plants left on earth.

❀ SPECIAL TREES ❀

Native and Introduced

Kaua'i's wet climate and fertile soil engender a tree-rich landscape, populated with notable Hawaiian trees such as–koa *(acacia koa),* 'ōhi'a lehua *(metrosideros polymorpha),* kukui *(aleurites moluccanus),* milo *(thespesia populnea),* and the kamani *(calophyllum inophyllum).* With the exception of 'ōhi'a lehua and koa, these trees were brought by early Polynesian settlers as essential components for their island lifestyle. Here is a more comprehensive list of trees found on Kaua'i:

Albizia–Introduced from Indonesia for reforestation, this tree has become extremely invasive and is the fastest growing tree on the planet.

Autograph tree–Found in dry places, you can scratch a message on this tree's thick leaves.

Banyan–Widespreading, with roots that hang from its branches.

Barringtonia–The fish poison tree. Hawaiians would use the pulp from its seeds to stun fish.

Calabash tree–Gourds for hula rattles.

Chinaberry (Pride of India)–Wood for hula instruments.

Christmas berry–Heavy, brushy growth found along roads.

Coconut–For food and drink and many useful purposes: roofing, screens, baskets, hats, mats, liquor. Coconut tree trimming is a booming business on Kaua'i.

Eucalyptus–From Australia; prevents erosion of soil and is useful for lumber, paper, pulp, essential oils, solvents, and perfumes; attracts honey bees. The trees are employed as windbreaks and for ornamental use.

Kamani–A scared Polynesian tree. Oil from the nuts is used for lamps, medicines, waterproofing, paint, lacquer.

Kamani, false–Found along shorelines; leaves turn red and yellow. Kamani nuts taste like almonds.

Kiawe (mesquite)–Introduced in 1828 by a Catholic priest; grows along coastlines in dry, hot areas. The wood is amazing for smoking and barbecuing, and kiawe blossoms are a great source for honey

Koa–The most valuable wood produced in Hawai'i. Its prized hardwood is used in making canoes, surfboards, 'ukuleles, furniture, and carvings.

Kou–Recently discovered to be indigenous to Hawai'i, it's used to make food dishes and containers because the wood is flavorless. A brown to red dye for kapa can be made from its dried leaves.

Kukui (candlenut)–Polished kukui nuts are used as ornaments and leis. The oil was once exported for use in paints and as an oil-based candle, and kukui nuts were used as a laxative.

Monkeypod–Large, common, umbrella-shaped tree; its wood is used for furniture and carvings.

Norfolk Island Pine–Symmetrical evergreen that grows upwards of 150 feet. Commonly used as a Christmas Tree in Hawai'i; planted with stands of coconuts in the past by navigators to replace masts on ships.

'Ōhi'a lehua–A very hard native wood with red poof blossoms; habitat for many native bird species. Makes fantastic posts, flooring, and furniture.

'Opiuma (Manila tamarind)–Called 'Opiuma when introduced to Hawai'i because of its black, opium-esque seeds. Used for lei making, lumber, dye, and as a bark-based gum.

Palms–Over 1,500 species in Hawai'i; coconut, date, fan, queen, and royal varietals.

© Ritu Jethani | Dreamstime.com

Paper bark–Named after its peeling, paper-like bark; has small white flowers. Used for thatching and soil erosion control; its leaf oil for medicinal use.

Sandalwood–Nearly extinct. Historically deforested for export of its fragrant wood to be used as incense, perfumes, chests, and furniture.

Tree fern (Hāpu'u, or 'i'i)–Grows in rainforests. The young fronds are edible; soft reddish-brown fiber (pulu) used to check bleeding and for embalming. Exported for pillows and mattresses in the 1800s. Its wood is used in growing orchids.

❀ POLYNESIAN PLANTS ❀

Canoe Plants

'Ape (Elephant's ear)–Famine food; antidote for itches.

'Awa (Kava)–An intoxicant is made from its roots.

'Awapuhi kuahiwi (Shampoo ginger)–A ginger plant with a tightly wrapped red bulbous flower; produces a sap-like substance when squeezed; natural soap or shampoo.

Hau–A type of hibiscus; extremely useful. It was kapu (forbidden) to harvest in historic times without consent by the royalty; strong cordage.

Ipu (Gourd)–Containers, musical instruments used in hula.

Kalo (Taro)–One of Kaua'i's most important plants. The mythological origin of Hawaiian people; the main crop staple of ancient Hawaiians; grown in flooded agricultural paddies.

Kamani *(Alexandrian laurel)*–Not to be mistaken with false Kamani. Introduced by Polynesian settlers; a red hardwood used for poi bowls, canoes, house building, trays. Low wood flavor; good for food purposes.

Ki (Ti)–Green leaf variety; sacred, it keeps away evil spirits from homes; good luck. A liquor, ʻōkolehao, is made from its roots. The leaves are used for cooking laulau, hula skirts, wrappers, thatch, lei, footwear, and for decorations.

Kō (Sugar cane)–Energy source for ocean voyages. Once Kauaʻi's largest import; sugar industry had ceased production on Kauaʻi.

Kukui (Candlenut)–A light source, its oil was used in stone dish lamps; the nuts strung on coconut fibers were used as candles, and stuffed in bamboo to be used as torches. The bark was used to dye tapa and as fish nets. Baby food was made from ground kukui nuts mixed with poi; mouthwash from sap. The oil from green nuts was used as a muscle relaxant and a laxative made from one to three green nuts.

Maiʻa (banana)–Matures in fourteen months; one bunch of bananas per tree. Propagated through "keiki" banana, small offshoots at the base of the tree.

Milo (Portia tree)–Now rare, they were used for cordage, utensils, furniture, jewelry, tanning, dye, oil, medicines and gum. Poi bowls called ‘umeke ‘ai were made from milo wood.

Niu (Coconut)–The best coconut water comes from young, green coconuts. Coconut meat was eaten as food, dried, and squeezed to make coconut milk.

Noni–A bitter, medicinal fruit high in enzymes. Its leaves are used for tea, and it's thought to have healing properties.

‘Ohe (Bamboo)–Used to make boat parts, containers, fishing equipment, food, furniture, hats, tools, mats, and musical instruments. A fast growing plant; recorded growing 47.6 inches in 24 hours.

‘Ōhi‘a ‘ai (Mountain apple)–Not a true apple, this pink and white fruit is juicy and crunchy.

‘Ōlena (Turmeric)–Used as an anti-inflammatory; traditionally a spiritual purifier.

‘Olonā–High strength white fibers used for cordage; now rare.

Pia (Polynesian arrowroot)–Starchy fiber; cooked like tapioca.

'Uala (Sweet potato)–Easy to grow, high-yielding fruiter.

Uhi (Yam)–Traditional food that never became as popular in Hawai'i as in other parts of Polynesia.

'Ulu (Breadfruit)–Ripens October to March, weighs up to ten pounds; eaten baked, boiled, broiled, or glazed.

© Pornsak Paewlumfaek | Dreamstime.com

Wauke (Paper mulberry)–Bark used for cloth, ceremonial purposes, garments, bedding; iwi (bones) were wrapped in tapa cloth.

History

TIMELINE

5-6 million years ago	Waimea Volcanic Series begins. Main volcanic dome of island is formed.
3.5 million years ago	Kōloa Volcanics, which covers much of eastern Kaua'i, begins to form.
0.5 million years ago	Last known volcanic eruptions, eastern portion of island.
125-500,000 years ago	Three major sea level changes form lithified sand dunes of Pa'ā, Māhā'ulepū, Kīpū Kai area.
15-18,000 years ago	Sea level is about 300 feet lower all around Kaua'i.
2-4,000 years ago	Sea level is as much as six feet higher all around Kaua'i.

Pre-300 A.D.	Mythological Era.
800-1100	Discovery and settlement of Kaua'i and Ni'ihau. First voyaging canoes arrive from Nu'uhiwa-Marquesas. Simple irrigation, worship of god Kāne. Simple kapu system of laws.
1300	Second wave of migration, Tahitians settle at Wailua. Stricter kapu system, human sacrifice to gods introduced. Land divisions made. Mo'ikeha becomes ruler of Kaua'i.
1360	Voyages to and from South Pacific end. Puna and Kona become separate kingdoms. Era of civil wars.
1400-1600	Peaceful and fruitful era centered around reign of Manokalanipō. Kingdoms of Puna and Kona united.
1600-1690	Civil wars divide island.

1690-1824	Ruling chief lineage ends with exile of Kaumuali'i.
1778	Captain James Cook anchors off Waimea.
1780	Kaumuali'i born at Wailua birthstone.
1786	First merchant ships anchors off Kaua'i.
1792	Explorer Vancouver arrives at Waimea.
1796	Kaumuali'i becomes ruler of Kaua'i
1796	Kamehameha raises large force on at Wai'anae, O'ahu, to conquer Kaua'i. Fleet of canoes are turned back by rough seas.
1798	Debora Kapule, wife of Kaumuali'i born.
1805	Kamehameha assembles large force on O'ahu to conquer Kaua'i. Epidemic decimates warriors.
1810	Kaumuali'i cedes Kaua'i and Ni'ihau to Kamehameha.
1816	Kaumuali'i cedes sections of Kaua'i to Russian American Company.

1817	Russians flee from Kaua'i.
1819	Kamehameha dies, kapu system overthrown.
1820	First American Protestant missionaries arrive at Waimea.
1821	Kaumuali'i exiled on O'ahu.
1822	Ali'i from other islands take control of Kaua'i.
1824	Kaumuali'i dies in Honolulu. Rebellion by his son Humehume fails.
1831	Richard Charlton starts first cattle ranch.
1835	Ladd & Co. start first commercial sugar plantation in Hawai'i, at Kōloa.
1840	U.S. Exploring Expedition tours island.
1848	Great Mahele, or division of lands.
1849	Lihue Plantation is founded.
1850s	Chinese immigrant plantation laborers arrive.

1863	A.B.C.F.M. withdraws support for missionaries.
1864	Ni'ihau sold to Sinclair-Gay family.
1878	First Portuguese immigrant workers arrive.
1885	Japanese immigrant plantation workers arrive.
1880s	Kauai Telephone Co. is formed.
1893	Hawaiian Monarchy is overthrown.
1900	G.N. Wilcox brings first automobile to Kaua'i.
1903	Radio link from O'ahu to Nāwiliwili goes on air. Garden Island Newspaper founded by S. Sheba.
1905	Kaua'i County government established.
1906	Pineapple industry started at Lāwa'i.
	Wireless tower transmits first signal from Kaua'i.
	First motion picture shown.

1911	Telephone service available across the island.
1912	Nāwiliwili Bay chosen as main port.
1912-1914	Kaua'i "Belt Road" built from Waimea to Hā'ena.
1913	Waiahi Electric lights Līhu'e.
1914	Tom Gunn pilots first airplane flight over Kaua'i.
1920	First airplanes fly from O'ahu to Kaua'i, two seaplanes, one piloted by Charlie Fern. Mary Waterhouse Rice is first woman to register to vote.
1922	First commercial radio broadcast heard. First ship passengers to land at a Kaua'i dock arrive at Ahukini.
1923	Matson Navigation provides direct shipment of sugar and pineapple to mainland from Ahukini and Port Allen.

1924	Filipino sugar workers strike at Hanapēpē.
1925	Navy Commander John Rodgers and crew aboard seaplane towed into Nāwiliwili Harbor after landing in mid-ocean in first attempt to fly from mainland to Hawai'i.
1926	Statewide Mutual Telephone system goes online.
1927	Army establishes Burns Field at Hanapēpē.
1928	Stop sign ordinance enacted.
1929	First regularly scheduled commercial air flight.
1930	Nāwiliwili Harbor opens with arrival of ship *Hualalai.*
1931	Interisland and mainland telephone service begins.
1934	First Līhu'e airport opens and first airmail arrives.

1935	Hawaiian outrigger canoe racing revived.
1937	Eight-hour work day begins at plantations.
1938	Līhu'e streets given names. G.N. Wilcox Hospital opens.
1940	KTOH, first commercial radio station, goes on the air.
1941	Pearl Harbor is bombed, WWII begins.
1942	Kauai Volunteers formed to protect island.
	First regular mainland army units arrive.
1945	WWII ends, Kaua'i GIs return home.
1946	Major tsunami, originating in Aleutian Islands, strikes.
1949	Regular interisland steamship service ends.
1950	Modernized Lihue Airport opens.
1952	KGB airs first television broadcast.

1953	Coco Palms Resort opens, launches larger-scale tourism era.
1957	Tsunami does major damage to North Shore.
1958	Bright light seen from atomic blast at Johnston Island.
1959	Hawai'i admitted as a state. Tourist hotels planned at Kalapakī.
1960	Fifty percent of work force is agricultural-related.
1965	First Kaua'i serviceman killed in Vietnam.
1967	Navy's underwater range installed at Barking Sands.
1970	Tourism jobs now outnumber agricultural jobs.
1973	End of pineapple industry.
1974	Opposition to resort development voiced.

1975	Papaya industry launched on AmFac lands at Moloa'a.
1976	Guava trees planted on C. Brewer lands at Kīlauea.
1981	Kauai Stores, 131-year-old plantation store, closes.
1982	Hurricane Iwa strikes Kaua'i.
1984	First direct United Airlines flight arrives as tourism industry expands.
1986	Annual visitor count to Kaua'i tops one million.
1987	Luxury resort hotels open at Kalapakī, Princeville, and Po'ipū. Coffee planted at McBryde Sugar Co.
1992	Hurricane 'Iniki devastates Kaua'i.
1994	Ready access to Internet offered.
1996	Koloa Mill closes, sugar growing ends at Kōloa.

2000	New Millennium celebrated.
2006	Ka Loko Dam on Kaua'i's north shore gives way killing seven people. The landowner, retired car dealer Jimmy Pflueger, was accused of reckless endangerment and served seven months of mostly in-home confinement.
2011	Ebay founder, Pierre Omidyar, announces plans to build a dairy farm on the island of Kaua'i.
2014	Facebook founder Mark Zuckerberg purchases 700 acres of land on Kaua'i's north shore—Pīla'a Beach and Kahu'āina Plantation.
2016	Police find $1.6M worth of crystal meth in Kaua'i's biggest drug bust at a home in Hanamā'ulu.
2019	Ulupono Initiative, led by billionaire eBay founder Pierre Omidyar, drops its plans to start Hawaii Dairy Farm.

2019	A tour helicopter owned by Safari Helicopters crashes in Kōke'e killing all passengers and pilot. The accidents reignites public pressure on the FAA.
2021	Billionaire Frank VanderSloot buys more than 2,000 acres on Kaua'i's northeastern coast to raise cattle. Police Chief Todd Raybuck is caught on audio mocking people of Asian descent.
2022	Witnesses report seeing a large circular object floating over Kaua'i for several hours. Days later, national news reports China's ongoing use of spy balloons as surveillance.
Jan 2023	Visitor arrivals in Kaua'i rebound to pre-pandemic levels with 106,980 visitors, a 26 percent increase from January 2022 and a 0.8 percent improvement from January 2019.

THE HAWAIIAN FLAG

The Hawaiian flag may have flown for the first time inside the rock walls of the 1816-built fort at Pāʻulaʻula along the Waimea River mouth.

Scotland-born Captain Alexander Adams, who sailed ships owned by Kamehameha, anchored the brig *Kaahumanu* off Waimea Fort in March 1817. Adams raised the Hawaiian flag during a provisioning stop at Waimea on the way to trade sandalwood for China goods in Canton, China.

Adams wrote in his log, "Gave the King (Kaumualiʻi) our ensign to hoist in lieu of the Russian (flag)..."

At the time, the Russian American Company out of Sitka, Alaska, manned a trading post at the fort and flew the RAC flag.

There is a debate over who designed the first Hawaiian flag. The color and layout of the red and white stripes, with the Union Jack in its top corner, mirror the flag of the British East India Company flown in the early nineteenth-century.

The creation of a distinct Hawaiian flag, giving credence to the Hawaiian Islands as a trading nation, was needed in the China Trade Era for Kamehameha's ship to enter Canton Harbor.

A British navy flag, also similar to the Hawaiian flag, was given to Kamehameha by explorer George Vancouver in 1793. A similar British flag, if not the same one, was noted as still flying at Kamehameha's fort at Honolulu in 1808.

CAPTAIN COOK AND PRE-MISSIONARY WESTERNERS

Captain James Cook (1728-1779) led the British Navy's voyaging expedition that came upon Kaua'i while heading from a winter respite in Tahiti on the way to the Pacific Northwest. The goal was to discover a Northwest Passage from the Pacific to the Atlantic to cut down the travel time to the rich trading ports of China.

Instead, Cook and the crews of his ships *Discovery* and *Resolution* in late January, 1778, made the first documented Western discovery of the Hawaiian Islands. The first landing came at the shoreline of Waimea; exactly where is uncertain.

Cook died one year later during a skirmish with Hawaiian warriors at Ka'awaloa, a village on Kealakekua Bay in leeward Hawai'i Island.

The publication of Cook's journals of this third voyage to the Pacific Ocean, in London in 1784, included a map of Kaua'i and opened up the island, and Hawai'i, to the Western world.

The legacy today of Cook in Hawai'i is overshadowed by his men infecting the native Hawaiian people with venereal diseases. In the world of Western navigation Cook stands out as the naval officer who developed calculating longitude to a high degree of accuracy, making global trade routes safe and highly profitable.

Merchant ships in the China fur trade stopped at Kaua'i for provisions while sailing between China and the Pacific Northwest. Englishman merchant captain John Meares arrived in the fall of 1787. Meares invited Ka'iana, an ali'i from Kaua'i, to sail to China. In 1789 the ship *Columbia* anchored off Waimea to trade. Captain Robert Gray's *Columbia* was the first American ship to circumnavigate the globe.

Hawaiian men from Kaua'i soon gained a reputation as excellent sailors and were recruited to serve on trading ships and later whaling ships.

Sandalwood, a fragrant tree once commonly found on the hillsides and mountains of Kaua'i, brought about major changes to the island. The first sticks of sandalwood sent to China from Hawai'i are cited as being cut down from the slopes of Ni'ihau and Kaua'i. Sandalwood was highly prized by Chinese merchants. It was used to make aromatic furniture and as incense in Chinese temples.

SUGAR PLANTATIONS

The sugar plantations which once operated along the coast from Mānā to Kīlauea and Princeville, from the 1840s into the early twenty-first century, provided the economic and social foundation for modern day Kaua'i.

The sugar industry provided prosperity and a common lifestyle for the majority of Kaua'i residents. Beginning in the 1850s, the sugar plantation owners provided a gateway for settlement on Kaua'i for tens of thousands of immigrant laborers and entrepreneurs from Asia, Europe, the Pacific Islands, and the Caribbean. Many of these immigrants chose to stay and settle in Kaua'i alongside the native Hawaiian and kama'āina Western families of Kaua'i and forever changed the ethnic makeup and mainstream lifestyle of the island.

❀ MAJOR SUGAR PLANTATIONS ❀

Koloa Plantation (Ladd & Company), founded in 1835, was the first commercial sugar plantation to grow and export sugar from Hawai'i; as McBryde Sugar, it closed in 1996.

Lihue Plantation Co. was established in 1849 on over 2,000 acres of land in and around Līhu'e; owned by Am-Fac/JMB; operation shut down in 2000.

Princeville Plantation was founded in 1861 along the Hanalei River and closed in the late nineteenth-century.

Grove Farm Co. established near Līhu'e in the mid-1850s as a sugar grower, sent its sugar cane to be milled elsewhere. Grove Farm leased its sugar growing lands in 1974 and entered the land development business.

McBryde Sugar Co. established in 1870 as Eleele Plantation before becoming McBryde Plantation at Numila, ceasing operations in 1996.

Kilauea Sugar. Co., established 1877 on a plantation founded by Charles Titcomb, closed in 1973.

Makee Sugar Co. grew sugar at Kapa'a and Kealia, combined operations with Lihue Plantation in 1933.

Hanamaulu Sugar Co., established 1877 by A.S. Wilcox, sold to Lihue Plantation in the 1910s.

Hawaiian Sugar Co. was established at Makaweli between McBryde Sugar and Kekaha Sugar in 1889 on land leased from the Gay and Robinson family. In 1889 Alexander & Baldwin took over the lease on the land. Hawaiian Sugar closed in 1941 to Olokele Sugar.

Gay & Robinson, the smallest sugar plantation in Hawai'i, was established at Makaweli in early 1880s by the Sinclair and Gay families. Gay & Robinson ground at Olokele Sugar. Olokele Sugar Co. at Makaweli. Gay & Robinson began operating Olokele in 1994 and closed operations in 2008.

Kehaha Sugar Co. established about 1880 by G.N. Wilcox, Paul Isenberg, Valdemar Knudsen, and Francis Sinclair on Knudsen land at Kekaha. Operations ended in 2000.

Waimea Sugar Mill Co., established 1884 by the Fayé family, closed plantation in 1969.

PRINCE KŪHIŌ

The most notable Kaua'i ali'i of its Territorial Era was Prince Jonah Kūhiō Kalaniana'ole Pi'ikoi (1871-1922).

Prince Kūhiō Park along the coast of Kōloa is his birthplace. A monument at the park commemorates Kūhiō's life and his native Hawaiian heritage, and a Hawai'i state holiday held every March 26 commemorates his birth. The monument is located at a fishing village on Ho'ai Bay at the Kukui'ula Village section of Kōloa.

The roots of the ali'i nui bloodlines of Kūhiō date back to Kaumuali'i, his great-grandfather. King Kalākaua named Kūhiō a prince in 1883 and adopted his family into his royal 'ohana.

Kūhiō studied in San Mateo, California, and in Japan.

He supported Queen Lili'uokalani when the Hawaiian Kingdom was overthrown in 1893 and took part in a failed counterrevolution in 1895, drawing time in prison.

In 1896 he married Elizabeth Kahanu Ka'auwai, a daughter of Kaua'i ali'i.

Following the Annexation of Hawai'i by the United States, Kūhiō, after much political indecision, accepted the new government and was elected as the second Hawai'i delegate to the U.S. Congress, serving until his death in 1922.

In 1903, Kūhiō organized the Order of Kamehameha and later organized the Hawaiian Civic Club organization.

As a Republican in Congress, Kūhiō championed the Hawaiian Homes Commission Act of 1921, which still provides homesteads for Native Hawaiians.

Kūhiō died on January 7, 1922, and was given the last state funeral held for an ali'i. He is interred in the Mauna 'Ala, the Royal Mausoleum, in Honolulu.

KAUMUALI'I

Kaumuali'i (c. 1780-1824) served as the last mō'ī (ruler) of the kingdom of Kaua'i, ruling from both Waimea and Wailua. Born to the mō'ī Ka'eokulani and his wife Kamakahelei, a high ranking hereditary ruling chiefess of Kaua'i, at the Pohaku Ho'ohanau (royal birthstones) along the Wailua River near Holoholoku heiau. His grandfather was Kekaulike, a notable warrior-king of Maui.

Kaumuali'i was named mō'ī of Kaua'i and Ni'ihau at age sixteen following the death of Ka'eokulani at the battle of Nu'uanu on O'ahu. Sailors taught him conversational English. British explorer George Vancouver befriended Kaumuali'i and bestowed him the name George in honor of King George of Great Britain.

The major problem of his years ruling Kaua'i was the threat of invasion by the military forces of Kamehameha

I and Kamehameha II Liholiho. In 1810, Kaumuali'i ceded Kaua'i to Kamehameha at an auspicious meeting in Honolulu. However, in 1816 Kaumuali'i was offered the assistance of the Czar of Russia in combating Kamehameha after he allowed a trading post at Pā'ula'ula (the site of the Russian Fort Elizabeth) to opened by the Russian American Company of Sitka, Alaska. But after working with the RAC party for a year, upon opposition from Kamehameha, Kaumuali'i ousted them from Kaua'i.

Kaumuali'i gladly approved the breaking of the 'ai kapu by the ali'i nui in 1819 and welcomed the American Protestant missionary party that arrived on Kaua'i in the spring and summer of 1820. Kaumuali'i later became a Christian under the influence of Keōpūolani, the sacred queen of Kamehameha.

In 1821, Liholiho sailed Kaumuali'i into exile from Waimea to Honolulu. In a diplomatic marriage, binding his leeward islands kingdom with the windward islands kingdom of the Kamehameha family, Kaumuali'i married Ka'ahumanu, a widow of Kamehameha and kuhina nui (regent) of Kamehameha's kingdom.

Kaumuali'i died in Honolulu in May, 1824, at about the age of 45. At his request, he was given a Christian burial in Lahaina, Maui, at the Waine'e (today Waiola) Church graveyard, in a tomb adjacent to the grave of Keōpūolani, the sacred queen of Kamehameha who died in Lahaina in 1823.

MOKU—TRADITIONAL HAWAIIAN DISTRICTS

Native Hawaiians living in Kaua'i dwelt in five distinct moku (major land sections).

Nā Pali (northwest): Deep "hanging" valleys due to coastline collapse, rich in kalo growing, almost impassable ridges, interior trails, fishing during calm ocean months.

Halele'a (north shore): Rainy, fertile valleys at Wainiha, Lumaha'i, and Hanalei; large scale kalo fields supported large population.

Ko'olau (northeastern corner): Smaller streams, kalo growing, dense population.

Puna (east side): Fertile lands along Wailua and Hulē'ia rivers, kalo-growing. The Wailua River basin, a sacred area of the ali'i; alternated with Waimea as capital of the island.

Kona (west side): From Polihale on north to border of Kōloa on east. Arid Waimea Valley rich in kalo growing, unique irrigation system at Menehune Ditch.

IMMIGRANT SUGAR WORKERS

1820s Chinese men arriving on Western merchant ships plant small fields of sugar cane at Kōloa; using handmade mill and boiling pans, produce processed sugar.

1852 Chinese contract workers immigrating from China hired as sugar workers at plantations in Hanalei, Kōloa, and Līhu‘e.

1853 German workers sought as managers for Kaua‘i sugar plantations. By 1899 over 800 Germans had arrived.

1868 A small group of contract Japanese plantation workers arrive, watched over by Japanese government concerned about their welfare.

1878 Portuguese immigrant workers arrive from Madeira and Azores islands. By 1888, 480 Portuguese were working on Kaua‘i plantations. Many luna foremen working in sugar fields were among these immigrants.

1880 Norwegians and other European immigrants

arrive as the Royal Agricultural Society seeks skilled workers for island plantations.

1883 The Kingdom of Hawai'i restricts Chinese immigration creating an opening for large-scale immigration of plantation workers from Japan and Okinawa.

1885 The Kanyaku Imin, the first large group of Japanese immigrant contract workers sent to Hawai'i, arrive in Honolulu; some sail to Kaua'i to work on plantations during a boom era for the Hawai'i sugar industry.

1900 Chinese immigration is halted when Hawai'i becomes a Territory of the United States.

1901 Japanese workers made up the majority of sugar plantation workers.

1903 Korean plantation workers sent to Kaua'i in limited numbers.

1906 The Hawaiian Islands and the Philippines are both American territories allowing Filipino plantation workers to be recruited, mostly arriving from the Locos Norte district of Luzon Island. Workers from the Visayan province also arrive.

KAUA'I AND THE OVERTHROW OF THE HAWAIIAN MONARCHY

The monarchy of the Kingdom of Hawai'i was overthrown in January, 1893. Due to Kaua'i's capital in Līhu'e being some ninety nautical miles from the rapidly evolving events in Honolulu, no response happened on the island during the week of the overthrow.

Lili'uokalani, the dethroned queen, did take a tour of Kaua'i in the summer of 1891 following the death of her predecessor King Kalākaua after her coronation. Missionary son, Kaua'i leader, and governor William Hyde Rice greeted her delegation. A lū'au was held at Rice's home near Nāwiliwili, attended by over 2,000 Kauaians. Lili'uokalani toured the island and Ni'ihau accompanied by Kōloa-born Prince Jonah Kūhiō Kalaniana'ole.

George Norton Wilcox of Kaua'i became Lili'uokalani's Minister of the Interior in October 1892 as part of an attempt to save her throne. But Wilcox and his cabinet resigned in January 1893 when a conflict broke out between the Royalists backing the queen and those who wished to restrict her power. Wilcox played no role in the overthrow of the monarchy.

On January 14, the queen announced plans to enforce a new constitution. A Committee of Safety then moved to overthrow Lili'uokalani. Serving on this committee were Albert Wilcox, the brother of G.N. Wilcox, who was a legislative representative from Kaua'i, and William O. Smith, a Kaua'i legislator, who used his Honolulu office as the headquarters for the Committee of Safety. The queen retracted her demand for a new constitution, but spoke out too late to avoid the overthrow of the monarchy.

Albert Wilcox helped Sanford B. Dole when Dole served as the first president of the Republic of Hawai'i. Dole's father had run a school at Kōloa for missionary children that Sanford attended as a youth.

Some Kaua'i leaders supported removing Lili'uokalani instead placing Princess Ka'iulani as queen.

During an attempted counter-revolution of Royalists in 1895, a quasi-military force called the Citizens Guard was formed. For several years Kaua'i was divided into two Guard districts–the Eastside, based in Līhu'e, and the Westside, based at Makaweli. Rifles and ammunition were supplied by the Republic of Hawai'i.

KAUA'I'S GOVERNMENT AFTER THE OVERTHROW

The Organic Act of 1900 resulted in Hawai'i becoming a Territory following its annexation by the United States in 1898. Early Territorial elections gave Native Hawaiians political control of all elective offices. In 1902 Kaua'i-born Republican Congressional candidate Prince Jonah Kūhiō Kalaniana'ole was elected to Congress and served until his death in 1922.

The County Act of 1905 divided the Territory of Hawai'i into five counties including Kaua'i County, which included Ni'ihau Island.

A great benefit for Kaua'i upon becoming a U.S. Territory was the federal financing for its first U.S. Post Office (at Līhu'e in 1901), paving of a belt-road, construction of harbors, and eventually airports.

The landmark County Building in Līhu'e was built in 1914. County government was ruled by an elected board of supervisors beginning in 1905. In 1969, Antone Vidinha became Kaua'i's first elected mayor.

The Kaua'i County government was founded on laws long used for local governance in the mainland United States.

This gave island citizens a much larger say in local government and finalized the transition of Kaua‘i and Ni‘ihau from rule under a constitutional monarchy to a republican form of government with democratic elections.

KAUA‘I MISSIONARIES

American Protestant Missionaries

On May 3, 1820, American Protestant missionary teacher Samuel Ruggles and teacher/mechanic Samuel Whitney landed at Waimea. With the missionaries aboard the brig *Thaddeus* out of Boston was Humehume (George Kaumuali‘i), son of Kaumuali‘i, the mō‘ī (ruler) of Kaua‘i. Kaumuali‘i invited the missionaries to establish a missionary station, promising land for a church, school, and homes.

On July 24, the two missionaries returned to Waimea with their wives, Nancy Wells Ruggles and Mercy Partridge Whitney. They first lived near Pā‘ula‘ula where the Russian American Company once manned a rock wall fort. Maria Kapule Whitney, the Whitneys' daughter, is believed to be the first Western child born on Kaua‘i. The Whitneys spent the rest of their lives at Waimea.

In 1832, a missionary station was established at Wai‘oli at Hanalei; a station at Kōloa where Kaua‘i's first Western

© Raycan | Dreamstime.com

doctor lived. The island's first school for Western children was started at Kōloa by missionary Daniel Dole in 1855.

Schools taught by native Hawaiian teachers who were trained by the missionaries opened around the island, including Kalalau Valley and other isolated areas. This brought literacy to almost all of Kaua'i's people.

Catholic Mission

St. Raphael the Archangel Church, the first Western-style Catholic church building on Kaua'i, was completed in 1856 on a seventeen-acre parcel outside of Kōloa town. In 1841, Father Arsenius Robert Walsh, an Irish priest of the Sacred Hearts order, celebrated the first known Catholic Mass on Kaua'i on Christmas Day, 1841, at Kōloa Landing. Catholic churches later opened at Hanalei, Moloa'a, Ni'ihau, and beyond.

Episcopal Mission

In 1864, Robert Crichton Wyllie, Foreign Minister of the Hawaiian Kingdom and founder of Princeville, advised Episcopal Bishop T.N. Staley to send the Rev. J.J. Elkington to Kaua'i. Elkington led services at Hanalei but returned to Honolulu. In 1881, Episcopal services were held at Kapa'a and All Saints Episcopal Church was formed.

Latter-Day Saints Mission

Latter-day Saints missionaries from the pioneer Mormon missionary party left for Hawai'i from the gold fields of California in December, 1850. Latter-day Saints missionaries William Farrer and John Dixon landed at Nāwiliwili and were opposed by the local American Protestant Mission and the Catholic Church. J.W.H. Kauwahi of Kaua'i helped translate and revise the Book of Mormon, and the final revision was completed at Waimea in 1854. The pioneer LDS mission later focused on settling on Lāna'i prior to the establishment of the LDS church on Kaua'i.

Buddhist Missions

The first large-scale immigration of Japanese sugar workers to Hawai'i in 1885 was seen as short-term. But many Japanese immigrants and their families chose to stay. By 1900, Buddhist organizations in Japan were sending priests to Kaua'i to establish temples. Hongwanji and Jodo Buddhist missions began at Keālia in 1899, at Līhu'e in 1901, at Kōloa in 1903, at Kīlauea in 1906, and at Waimea in 1908.

PRE-WESTERN NATIVE HAWAIIAN LIFE

The First Settlers

Archaeology, language studies, and DNA analysis point to the homeland of the early settlers of Kaua'i as the islands of eastern Polynesia, now known as French Polynesia. The first voyaging canoes probably sailed from Nu'uhiwa (the Marquesas Islands in French Polynesia). Material clues to this belief include Marquesan-style ring and stirrup topped basalt poi pounders found only on Kaua'i in the Hawaiian Islands.

The legendary Menehune of Kaua'i may have been settled here when the first Polynesian voyaging canoes landed on a Kaua'i beach.

Early Polynesian settlers clustered along the coast near streams and rivers where the environment was good for fishing and agriculture. Archaeological materials dated to about 1000 A.D. have been found in kalo (taro) fields in Hanalei Valley. Artifacts found by Bishop Museum archaeologists at Nu'alolo Kai at Na Pali date to about 1200 A.D.

Tahitian warriors and settlers came to Hawai'i from central Polynesia around 1200-1300 A.D. Pā'ao, a priest from Ra'iatea, a leeward Tahitian island, introduced human sacrifice. Voyaging south was cut off in Pā'ao's time. Following this era there is no known evidence of contact with the Polynesian Islands to the south until the arrival of British explorer Captain James Cook in 1778.

Legendary Rulers

Tahiti and Ra'iatea islands are key locations in the story of the early ali'i rulers of Kaua'i.

Mo'ikeha was a legendary voyager and ruler of Tahitian lineage. After adventuring in Waipi'o Valley in windward Hawai'i island, and at Ra'iatea, the sacred island of French Polynesia, Mo'ikeha sailed to the shores of Wailua around 1100-1200 A.D. Mo'ikeha was known as a handsome man who attracted Ho'oipo-i-ka-malanai, the daughter of Puna, the mō'ī (king) of Kaua'i. The couple married and when Puna died, Mo'ikeha became ruler. The couple had three sons who each became a ruling chief on Kaua'i, on O'ahu, and Hawai'i island. Mo'ikeha's name translates as "great king."

La'amaikahiki (La'a-from-Tahiti) was the son of Mo'ikeha by his Tahitian wife Lu'ukia. La'a sailed from Ra'iatea to Wailua. La'a is notable in Hawaiian lore for introducing the pahu drum. Carved from a tall hollow log and covered at one end with a shark skin, the pahu was first drummed at the Kalaeokamanu (The Crest of the Bird) heiau overlooking the Wailua River. Today the pahu drum is a key instrument in modern hula performances.

Ahukinia-La'a, one of La'a's three sons, ruled Kaua'i. Ahukini Landing along Hanamā'ulu Bay is named after Ahukinia-La'a.

Manokalanipō was a legendary king of Kaua'i born at Wailua about 1350. Through focusing on developing great agriculture projects and keeping peace, he brought generations of calm and prosperity to Kaua'i and Ni'ihau in a time known as the "Golden Era" of Kaua'i. So great was his rule that Kaua'i became known as "Kaua'i-a-Manokalanipō."

Sources

Unique Kaua'i

Kaua'i Forest Bird Recovery Project. "Our Mission." Kaua'i Forest Bird Recovery Project, n.d., https://kauaiforestbirds.org/missionbackground/

Hawaii Department of Land and Natural Resources, Division of Forestry and Wildlife. "Welcome to DOFAW." DOFAW, n.d., https://dlnr.hawaii.gov/dofaw/

Kaua'i Statistics

"Niihau CCD, Kauai County, Hawaii". census.gov. United States Census Bureau

Kaua'i's People

United States Census Bureau. "Kauai County, Hawaii: Race and Hispanic Origin." 2010 Census Summary File 1. U.S. Census Bureau, 2010, factfinder.census.gov/bkmk/table/1.0/en/DEC/10_SF1/QTP5/0500000US15007. Accessed 6 April 2023

Religions

U.S. Census Bureau QuickFacts: Kauai County, Hawaii." Census Bureau QuickFacts, United States Census Bureau, 1 July 2021, https://www.census.gov/quickfacts/kauaicountyhawaii

County Membership Report - Kauai County, Hawaii (HI)." Association of Religion Data Archives, The ARDA, www.thearda.com/rcms2010/r/c/15/rcms2010_15007_county_name_2010.asp

The Church of Jesus Christ of Latter-day Saints Membership Statistics." Newsroom of The Church of Jesus Christ of Latter-day Saints, 2021, newsroom.churchofjesuschrist.org/facts-and-statistics/country/united-states/state/hawaii

Precious Lands

U.S. Census Bureau. "United States Quick Facts: Kauai County, Hawaii." 2021. https://www.census.gov/quickfacts/kauaicountyhawaii

United States Department of Agriculture Forest Service. "Hawaii Forest Resource Assessment." USDA Forest Service, Pacific Southwest Region, 2021, https://www.fs.usda.gov/naspf/sites/default/files/2021-04/hawaii.pdf

National Agricultural Statistics Service (NASS). "Hawaii Land Use 2019." nass.usda.gov, 2020, https://www.nass.usda.gov/Publications/Todays_Reports/reports/land0819.pdf

Department of Hawaiian Home Lands. DHHL Annual Report FY 2020, 2021, https://dhhl.hawaii.gov/wp-content/uploads/2021/03/DHHL-Annual-Report-FY-20.pdf

Hawaii State Department of Business, Economic Development & Tourism. State of Hawaii Data Book 2020: Land Area, Ownership, and Use, Table 1.43, p. 55 https://files.hawaii.gov/dbedt/economic/databook/db2020/section06.pdf

"KAUAI LANDOWNERS MAP" Kauai Landowners Map, 10 April, 2023 https://www.cccarto.com/hawaiiproperty/kauai

Hawaii Statewide GIS Program, Hawaii Department of Business, Economic Development & Tourism. (n.d.). Kauai Landowners. Retrieved April 12, 2023, from https://files.hawaii.gov/dbedt/op/gis/maps/kauai_large_landowners.pdf

Large Landowners Tables 2013 (Corrected)." Hawaii State Department of Business, Economic Development & Tourism, n.d., files.hawaii.gov/dbedt/op/gis/data/large_landowners_tables_2013_corrected.xls

Agriculture

Center for Food Safety. "Can the Seed Industry's Decline Lead to a Sustainable Food System?" Center for Food Safety, 15 Feb. 2022, https://www.centerforfoodsafety.org/blog/5748/can-the-seed-industrys-decline-lead-to-a-sustainable-food-system

Ernst, Cheryl. "New Big 5 May Be Emerging in Hawaii." Hawaii Business Magazine, 7 April 2013, https://www.hawaiibusiness.com/new-big-5-may-be-emerging-in-hawaii/

Harn R.O. Systems. "Which Takes More Water to Produce: A Pound of Beef or a Pound of Corn?" Harn R.O. Systems Blog, 23 May 2018, https://blog.harnrosystems.com/which-takes-more-water-to-produce-a-pound-of-beef-or-a-pound-of-corn

Hawaii Department of Agriculture. "Taro Statistics 2021." State of Hawaii, 31 Oct. 2022, https://hdoa.hawaii.gov/wp-content/uploads/2022/11/Taro-Stats-2021_SOH_10.31.2022R.pdf

Hawaii Department of Agriculture. "Hawaii Agricultural Baseline 2020 Update: Hawaii, Kauai, Maui, and Honolulu Counties." January 2022, hdoa.hawaii.gov/wp-content/uploads/2022/01/2020_Update_Ag_Baseline_all_Hawaiian_Islands_v5.pdf

Johnson, Renée. "Mergers in Seeds and Agricultural Chemicals: What Happened?" *Amber Waves,* vol. 17, no. 1, Feb. 2019, https://www.ers.usda.gov/amber-waves/2019/february/mergers-in-seeds-and-agricultural-chemicals-what-happened/

"Kauai Coffee Company." Kauai Coffee Company, https://kauaicoffee.com/pages/about-kauai-coffee-company Accessed 13 Apr. 2023

Kauai Visitors Bureau. (2021). Kauai Cattle Ranching. Retrieved from https://www.kauai.com/blog/kauai-cattle-ranching

Loomis, Ilima. "Hawaii Business Environmental Report: Pesticides." *Hawaii Business Magazine,* 20 May 2016, https://www.hawaiibusiness.com/hawaii-business-environmental-report-pesticides/

Parachini, Allan. "Kauai: Why the Beef Industry Is Rapidly Expanding on the Garden Island." Civil Beat, 19 June 2018, https://www.civilbeat.org/2018/06/kauai-why-the-beef-industry-is-rapidly-expanding-on-the-garden-island/

Schnitkey, Gary. "Corn and Soybean Yields in 2022." farmdoc daily, Department of Agricultural and Consumer Economics, University of Illinois at Urbana-Champaign, 10 Jan. 2023, https://farmdocdaily.illinois.edu/2022/12/corn-and-soybean-yields-in-2022.html

United States Department of Agriculture. "Hawaii Seed Crops – 1998." National Agricultural Statistics Service, 1999, https://www.nass.usda.gov/Statistics_by_State/Hawaii/Publications/Archive/Seeds/xsee98.pdf

United States Department of Agriculture. "2019 and 2020 Hawaii County Data." National Agricultural Statistics Service, 21 Jan. 2021, https://www.nass.usda.gov/Quick_Stats/Ag_Overview/stateOverview.php?state=HAWAII

Cost of Living

https://www.bestplaces.net/cost_of_living/county/hawaii/kauai

https://www.bestplaces.net/cost_of_living/county/hawaii/kauai

https://dbedt.hawaii.gov/economic/qser/county/

Visiting Kaua'i

https://files.hawaii.gov/dbedt/economic/databook/db2021/section07.pdf

https://files.hawaii.gov/dbedt/economic/databook/db2021/section23.pdf

How Far from Home?

https://www.distance.to/Kauai

www.travelmath.com

Weather

Ahrens, C.D. (2000), Meteorology Today, Brooks/Cole, ISBN 0-534-39776-X

"In The Wake of Water: Kauai." Cook, Christian

FLUX Hawaii, 24 Apr. 2018, fluxhawaii.com/in-the-wake-of-water-kauai/ Accessed 16 April 2023

Piercy, LaRue. *Hawaii This and That.* Mutual Publishing, 2006

Favorite Attractions

Hawaii Tourism Authority. 2019 Annual Report. Hawaii Tourism

Authority, 2020, https://www.hawaiitourismauthority.org/media/5062/2019-annual-report-final-for-posting.pdf

Hawaii Tourism Authority. "February 2023 Visitor Statistics." Hawaii Tourism Authority, Feb. 2023, https://www.hawaiitourismauthority.org/media/10793/february-2023-visitor-statistics-final-002.pdf

"Kauai Visitor Demographics." Kauai Travel Blog, 13 May 2020, https://www.kauaitravelblog.com/kauai-visitor-demographics/

"Top 10 places tourists visited on Kauai in 2021." KHON2, 20 August 2021, https://www.khon2.com/local-news/top-10-places-tourists-visited-on-kauai-in-2021/

Hawaiian Holidays and Celebrations

Kanahele, George S. *Emma, Hawai'i's Remarkable Queen: A Biography.* Honolulu: University of Hawaii Press, 1999

Whitton, Kevin. "Hawaii Travel Guide." Moon Travel, 2018.

Free Kaua'i Entertainment

https://kauaifestivals.com/festival/old-kapaa-town-1st-saturday-art-walk/2023-04-01/

"Koke'e State Park–Festivals–Emalani." Koke'e State Park, State of Hawaii Department of Land and Natural Resources, www.kokee.org/index.php?festivals-emalani Accessed 17 Apr. 2023

Music of the Heart

"Biography." IZ Hawaii, Mountain Apple Company, 2023, https://izhawaii.com/biography/

"Carlos Andrade." Hokulea Archive, Polynesian Voyaging Society, 1985, https://archive.hokulea.com/carlos85.html

Cheape, Charlie. "Larry Rivera: Aloha Begins With Him." *The Garden Island,* 17 Sept. 2017, www.thegardenisland.com/2017/09/17/hawaii-news/larry-rivera-aloha-begins-with-him/

"Obituary for Tuesday, August 16, 2022." *The Garden Island,* 16 Aug. 2022, https://www.thegardenisland.com/2022/08/16/

obituaries/obituary-for-tuesday-august-16-2022/#:~:text=Carlos%20Lawrence%20Andrade,-Carlos%20Lawrence%20Andrade&text=He%20was%20born%20on%20May,a%20professor%2C%20musician%20and%20waterman

Warmstrong, Kathryn. "Larry Rivera and Elvis Presley: Choosing the Slow Life." God's Word for Gardeners Bible, 1 Feb. 2017, https://kathrynwarmstrong.wordpress.com/2017/02/01/larry-rivera-and-elvis-presley-choosing-the-slow-life/

Kaua'i's Birds

Birds of Hawaii Info. "Red-crested Cardinal." Birds of Hawaii Info, https://www.birdsofhawaii.info/p/red-crested-cardinal.html.

Center for Biological Diversity. "Back from the Brink: Hawaii's Nene Goose a Recovery Success Story." Center for Biological Diversity, 8 Dec. 2019, https://biologicaldiversity.org/w/news/press-releases/back-from-the-brink-hawaiis-nene-goose-a-recovery-success-story-2019-12-08/

Kauai Forest Birds. "Meet the Birds." Kauai Forest Birds Recovery Project, https://kauaiforestbirds.org/meet-the-birds-2/.

Paxton, Eben H., et al. "Collapsing avian community on a Hawaiian island." Science Advances, vol. 2, no. 9, 7 Sept. 2016, https://www.science.org/doi/10.1126/sciadv.1600029

U.S. Fish & Wildlife Service. "Kilauea Point National Wildlife Refuge: Species List." U.S. Fish & Wildlife Service, https://www.fws.gov/refuge/kilauea-point/species.

Animals

"Hawaiian Bat–Hawai'i Volcanoes National Park." National Park Service, U.S. Department of the Interior, accessed 24 Apr. 2023, https://www.nps.gov/havo/learn/nature/hawaiian-bat.htm

Simmons, Nancy; Cirranello, A.L. (2020). "Bat Species of the World: A taxonomic and geographic database". Retrieved October 20, 2021

Native Plants

Bruegmann, M.; Caraway, V.L.; Clark, M. (2016). "Astelia waialealae". IUCN Red List of Threatened Species. 2016

Federal Register, vol. 85, no. 84, 30 Apr. 2020, pp. 23833-23958. https://www.govinfo.gov/content/pkg/FR-2020-04-30/pdf/2020-09177.pdf

Hawaii Department of Land and Natural Resources. "Fact Sheet: Viola kauaiensis var. wahiawaensis." n.d. https://dlnr.hawaii.gov/wildlife/files/2013/09/Fact-Sheet-Viola-kauaiensis-var-wahiawaensis.pdf

"Hibiscadelphus distans (Malvaceae)". *Meet the Plants.* National Tropical Botanical Garden

"NTBG Completes IUCN Red Listing for all Kauai endemic plants" National Tropical Botanical Garden, March 25, 2021 https://ntbg.org/news/ntbg-completes-iucn-red-listing-for-all-kauai-endemic-plants/

"The Kanaele Bog Preserve." The Nature Conservancy, n.d., https://www.nature.org/en-us/get-involved/how-to-help/places-we-protect/kanaele-bog/

USFWS. Determination of endangered status for 48 species on Kauai and designation of critical habitat. Federal Register April 13, 2010

Special Trees

"Albizia and Eucalyptus Trees Used to Restore Forests Damaged by Wildfire on the Sierra National Forest." USDA Forest Service, 2021, https://www.fs.usda.gov/detail/r5/home/?cid=FSEPRD998943

"Autograph tree: Clusia rosea" at "Hawaii's Most Invasive Horticultural Plants" at http://www.state.hi.us/dlnr/dofaw/hortweeds/species/cluros.htm

"Common Forest Trees of Hawaii (Native and Introduced)" Little, Elbert L. Jr., Skolmen, Roger G. United States Department of Agriculture Forest Service Agriculture Handbook No. 679 Washington, DC May 1989 https://www.fs.usda.gov/psw/publications/documents/misc/ah679.pdf

"Kou (Cordia subcordata)." Maui Nui Botanical Gardens, mnbg.org/hawaiian-native-plant-collection/kou-cordia-subcordata/ Accessed 25 April 2023

"Fish Poison Tree | Hawaii Tropical Botanical Garden." Hawaii Tropical Botanical Garden, https://htbg.com/barringtonia-asiatica-fish-poison-tree/

Nelson-Kaula, Kehauwealani; Ostertag, Rebecca; Flint Hughes, R; Dudley, Bruce D (Jul 2016). "Nutrient and Organic Matter Inputs to Hawaiian Anchialine Ponds: Influences of N-Fixing and Non-N-Fixing Trees"

Polynesian Plants

Abbott, Isabella Aiona; *La'au Hawai'i–Traditional Hawaiian Uses of Plants;* Bishop Museum Press, 1992

Lee, Pali and Koko Willis; *Tales From The Night Rainbow;* 1984

Miyano, Leland. *Hawaii's Beautiful Trees.* Mutual Publishing, 1997

Whistler, W. Arthur. *Plants of the Canoe People: An Ethnobotanical Voyage Through Polynesia.* National Tropical Botanical Garden, 2009